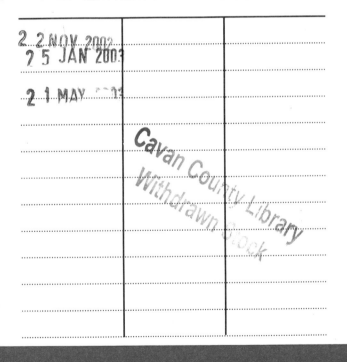

Titles in this series
Big J
Clever Cleo
Gunpowder Guy
Hal the Hero
The Little Queen
Will's Dream

Text copyright © Stewart Ross 2000
Illustrations copyright © Sue Shields 2000

Series concept: Stewart Ross
Series editor: Alex Woolf
Editor: Liz Gogerly
Book Design: Design Systems

The publisher would like to thank Michael Holford for kind permission to use the picture on page 30 from the Bayeux Tapestry/Harold's Oath to William.

A catalogue record for this book is available from the British Library.

ISBN 07502 2964 0

Printed and bound in Italy by G. Canale & C.S,p.A., Turin.

Published in Great Britain by Hodder Wayland,
a division of Hodder Children's Books

Hodder Children's Books
A division of Hodder Headline Limited

Will's Dream

Stewart Ross
Illustrated by Sue Shields

HODDER
Wayland

an imprint of Hodder Children's Books

Will was a great man.

He lived in France.

Will had a beautiful wife and many fine children.

He also had a great castle and lots of land.

But Will wanted more...

Will went to England.

Will wanted to be the next King of England.

And Edward wanted Will to be the next king.

Harold wanted to be the next king, too!

Will went back to France.

Later, old King Edward died.

Harold was the new king of England.

Will was very angry.

He had not got what he wanted!

Will asked soldiers to help him.

Will and his soldiers sailed to England.

Harold and his men came to meet Will.

They rested on a hill.

Will's soldiers charged up the hill...

...then charged down again!

Harold's soldiers ran after them.

Will's soldiers turned round and beat them up.

Harold was almost alone.

Soon it was all over.

At last, Will had everything...

...he wanted!

Do you know?

This story is TRUE!
Will was KING WILLIAM THE FIRST.
This can be written 'WILLIAM I'.
He is also called WILLIAM THE CONQUEROR.
William was king of England 950 years ago.
This is what he looked like:

Notes for adults

Will's Dream and the National Curriculum:
Will's Dream grew out of the ideas presented in two recent documents: the Department for Education and Employment's *National Literacy Strategy* and the Qualifications and Curriculum Authority's *Maintaining Breadth and Balance at Key Stages 1 and 2*. It is both a Key Stage 1 reader, offering stimulating material for use during the Literacy Hour, and a useful springboard for Key Stage 1 history. In presenting the story of William the Conqueror in the simplest possible terms, it introduces the child to one of the best-known figures from British history and presents many opportunities for (a) 'looking for similarities and differences between life today and in the past', (b) 'talking and writing about what happened and why people acted as they did', and (c) 'finding out about the past using different sources of information and representations'. (Maintaining Breadth and Balance, P10.)

Suggested follow-up activities

1. Checking the child knows and can use words they might not have come across before. In particular:

France	angry	goodbye	dream
England	castle	au revoir	quicker
bonjour	Edward	everyone	
beautiful	wanted	sailed	
French	Harold	Hastings	
happen	soldiers	charged	

2. Talking about things remaining from Norman times, e.g. buildings (Tower of London, other castles and cathedrals), The Domesday Book, the Bayeux Tapestry etc.

3. Discussing how we know about William the Conqueror, i.e. sources (perhaps starting with the Bayeux Tapestry).

4. Explaining the exact date of William's reign, (1066–1087), and what they mean.

5. Going further into aspects of William's reign, e.g. Edward the Confessor and Anglo-Saxon England, Normandy and France, the Norman Conquest, the rebellions, the influence of Norman French on our language, William's sons and the succession.

6. Comparing life in William's time with our own, e.g. clothing, sailing ships, travel, warfare.